DODD, MEAD WONDERS BOOKS include WONDERS OF:

Wonders of
Peacocks

Sigmund A. Lavine

Illustrated with photographs and old prints

DODD, MEAD & COMPANY
NEW YORK

For Linda

who has every reason to be as proud as . . .

ILLUSTRATIONS COURTESY OF: American Museum of Natural History, 44; Author's Collection, 23, 30 *bottom*, 37; British Museum, 20, 21, 29, 30 *top*; The British Tourist Authority, 61; Butterfield & Butterfield, 59; Field Museum of Natural History, 15, 34, 46; Hawaiian State Archives, 58; The Information Service of India, 43; Alan S. Maltz, *frontispiece*, 6, 8, 10, 35, 49, 52; Museum of Fine Arts, Boston, 25; © New York Zoological Society Photo, 17, 36, 56; Zoological Society of Cincinnati, Photo by John E. Moreau; © Zoological Society of San Diego, 54.

1   2   3   4   5   6   7   8   9   10

Library of Congress Cataloging in Publication Data

Lavine, Sigmund A.
    Wonders of peacocks.

    Includes index.
    Summary: Describes the three species of
iridescent-plumaged pheasants commonly known
as peacocks, and traces their influence on
folklore, religion, literature, and art.
    1. Peafowl—Juvenile literature. 2. Peafowl—
Folklore—Juvenile literature. [1. Peacocks]
I. Title.
QL696.G27L38   598'.617   82–4987
ISBN 0–396–08037–5   AACR2

Contents

1 The Peacock's Fan

"And stately peacocks with their splendid eyes."—Hood

Ornithologists—students of birds—insist that laymen are in error when they describe peacocks as large gallinaceous (fowl-like) birds whose brilliant plumage displays a dazzling pattern of iridescent blues, golds, and greens. According to the authorities, the word peacock should be used only to identify a male bird of the genera *Pavo* or *Afropavo*, despite the fact that common speech also applies the term to a female. Technically, the proper name for a female is peahen, while the accepted collective form is peafowl. Generally, these distinctions are ignored, except in scientific literature. This book follows the practice of common usage.

Few sights in nature are more magnificent than watching a male peacock unfold his richly colored, lacy fan of feathers. The elongated plumes of this fan, which form a train, may trail as much as five feet behind a mature bird. While a peacock's train glitters and shimmers in the sunlight when not

A male Indian peacock, popularly called the common or blue peacock

erect, it rivals "the splendor and jewel-like quality of Oriental treasure troves" when raised and spread.

Not only do lustrous metallic tints make an open fan a wondrous sight but also the multicolored spots scattered over the feathers add to its beauty. Because these spots resemble eyes, ornithologists call them ocelli (Latin for "little eyes"). Bird lovers are not so technical. They call ocelli "eyespots."

Despite popular opinion, a peacock's fan is not formed by long tail feathers. Actually, the train consists of strong-shafted, extremely long coverts—protective feathers that cover the quills in a bird's tail and wings. Extending far beyond the real tail of twenty light-brown feathers, each of the coverts has a conspicuous "eye" near its outer end. Because the coverts differ in length, the eyes are scattered over the train. When displaying, a peacock throws the coverts upward and unfolds them like a fan. While erect and spread, the coverts are supported by the much shorter tail feathers.

The peacock's enormous feathery fan may be a glorious sight but physicists who specialize in optics—the science treating of light—view it with scientific detachment. These experts, having determined that peacock plumage is mostly brown in hue, can prove that the splendor of the train is really an optical illusion caused by light striking the feathers from different angles and bringing out an array of colors ranging from copper, bronze, and gold to deep blue-green and violet.

However, when a peacock spreads its fan, few individuals besides physicists remember that the play of colors across the feathers is due to the refraction and reflection of light. Cold scientific fact cannot compete with the beauty of the sight. Similarly, while a peacock has been called a "glorified chicken,"

Side view of blue peacock with fan spread clearly shows the short tail quills below the long feathers or coverts.

A blue peacock with fan spread—a splendid sight

most laymen do not consider it poultry but an exotic creature.

Not only is the peacock the most impressive of all birds with iridescent plumage but also it is an outstanding example of a bird whose feathers have been modified for appearance only rather than to serve as protection against cold, or as an aid to flight.

Peacocks are polygamous. Each male tries to accumulate a harem of two to five hens. Thus, as soon as a male sees a female, he begins his display. Coverts raised, the male waits until the hen draws near and, when she does, madly beats his wings

10

as his feathery plumes spread outward into a conelike fan. Strutting proudly before the hen, the male suddenly moves toward her and gives a loud scream as he shivers so violently that his tail quills vibrate. Some individuals find the noise made by the vibrating quills very loud. On the other hand, there are those who hold that the quills rustle, "producing a soft penetrating sound like the patter of rain on dry leaves."

Incidentally, males do not display their outspread trains to potential mates exclusively. They may show their fan to any passing bird or to humans. In fact, naturalists have confirmed that peacocks display more often and for longer periods of time in front of groups of people than they do in the presence of hens. It well may be that the ancient belief is correct in stating peacocks are vain!

2 Meet the Peacocks

". . . the Blue Birds of impossible Paradise."—Smith

Peacocks and the majority of their relatives are known to zoologists as pheasants. Ornithologists have placed the pheasants in a family of birds called the Phasianidae. They compounded the term "Phasianidae" from Phasis, a river that winds through the Caucasian Mountains to the Black Sea. The reason for using Phasis as the root of a scientific name is that many early naturalists reported observing pheasants along its banks. Incidentally, wealthy Romans had also displayed great interest in these long-tailed, brilliantly colored birds. This was because they considered their flesh a great delicacy. In fact, cooks who devised new recipes for preparing *Phasianus avis* (the bird of the Phasis) were richly rewarded.

While all the Phasianidae are gallinaceous, they are a varied flock, consisting of the misnamed turkey, the noisy guinea hen, the valuable chicken, the colorful pheasants, and the gorgeous peacock.

Most of the Phasianidae are handsome birds. But none present a more spectacular appearance than the peacock. In fact, the sumptuous adornment of the bird's resplendent plumage

An old print shows some Phasianidae—guinea fowl (bottom left and center), blue peacock, and turkeys, domestic and (far right) wild.

along with its elegant manner have led to the peacock's being labeled "the most beautiful of birds." Even those who do not think the peacock deserves this title admit that they can appreciate why it has been admired for untold centuries. Such present-day praise for the peacock's beauty makes it easy to understand why, in ancient times, conquerors accepted it as tribute and kings considered the bird a worthy gift. No early rulers esteemed the peacock more highly than the Pharaohs of Egypt, who acquired numbers of the birds from Phoenician traders. These seafarers bought the birds in India and then sold them to royalty and wealthy men throughout the Mediterranean region.

Man's long association with the peacock is well documented. On the other hand, ornithologists admit that they cannot trace the bird's line of ancestry. However, fossils do reveal that huge

13

forebears of the Phasianidae lived during the Miocene period approximately a million years ago.

Because of the great scarcity of early bird fossils, paleontologists—students of fossils—do not have the necessary evidence to determine when the giant ancestors of the Phasianidae vanished and were replaced by smaller species that became the immediate progenitors of today's fowl-like birds. Nor can the experts trace the evolution of the peacock from this stock. Nevertheless, ornithologists are convinced that the peacock was flaunting its long train some fifty thousand years ago.

There are three species of peacock. The best known is the Indian peacock (*Pavo cristatus*). Popularly called either the blue or common peacock, *cristatus* lives in the dense jungles of India and the island of Sri Lanka.

The green peacock (*Pavo muticus*) has a more easterly distribution than the blue peacock. It is a native of Burma, Java, Malaysia, and Thailand. Not only is *muticus*—which many ornithologists hold to be the most beautiful and impressive of all the fowl-like birds—bedecked with plumage different from that of the blue peacock but also it is more streamlined than its Indian kin.

Undoubtedly, peacocks are the oldest known ornamental birds. But despite the fact that peacocks have been reared in captivity for more than four thousand years, the Congo peacock (*Afropavo congensis*) has been known to science only since 1936. Moreover, the chances are that *congensis*, a resident of the dense rain forests of Zaire (formerly the Belgian Congo), might have remained unnoticed indefinitely were it not for a feather in an African chieftain's headdress, a crowded museum, and a very curious naturalist.

The curious naturalist was Dr. James P. Chapin, the foremost authority on the birds of central Africa. While on an expedition

The spoon-shaped crest of the common or blue peacock, LEFT, *is composed of blue-tipped, brushlike feathers. The Javan or green peacock,* RIGHT, *is more streamlined than the blue peacock. As a result, it appears to be much larger.*

in 1913, Chapin made camp near an Ituri village deep in the rain forest. The villagers welcomed him with songs and dances, but Chapin paid little attention to the festivities. He was concentrating on the reddish-brown feather marked with black in the center of the headdress worn by the Ituri chief. But Chapin was unable to identify the feather.

Positive that he could determine the bird from which the feather had been plucked if he could examine it thoroughly, Chapin acquired the headdress. However, even looking at the feather through a magnifying glass gave him no clue to its source. Nor was the ornithologist able to name the feather on his return to New York City, where he compared it with countless specimens in the American Museum of Natural History. Frustrated, Chapin put the feather in a drawer.

Twenty-one years later, Chapin paid one of his frequent visits to the Royal Museum of Central Africa in Tervuren, a small town on the outskirts of Brussels. Late one afternoon, while walking down a dimly lit corridor, Chapin noticed, for the first time, two mounted birds about the size of roosters. Always curious, Chapin carried the birds to the nearest window, where he saw that one had blackish plumage with a green, bronze, and violet sheen while the other was reddish-brown and black with green-glossed underparts. Light from the window also enabled Chapin to read the tags on the birds' necks. They indicated that the specimens were immature green peacocks. Because they lacked the general appearance and coloration of immature green peacocks, Chapin knew immediately that the birds were mislabeled. Nevertheless, he was sure that they were peacocks.

Then, too, there was something familiar about the brown feathers of one of the birds. On a hunch, Chapin cabled his office in New York to send him the feather he had taken from the chief's headdress so long ago.

While waiting for the feather to arrive, Chapin learned that the mislabeled birds were the gift of an African trader who had sent them to the museum from the Congo. Because the museum was crowded with exhibits, the birds had been stored in the corridor where Chapin found them.

Eventually the feather reached Chapin and he compared it

Male Congo peacock. All Congo peacocks lack trains.

with those of one of the mounted birds. It was a perfect match. Convinced that a hitherto unknown peacock occurred in the Congo region, the ornithologist organized an expedition to find it. Once in Africa, Chapin took his group to the Ituri village where he had first seen the mysterious feather. This was because Chapin theorized that the feather had come from a bird native to the jungle surrounding the village. He was right. Within a few weeks, Chapin had found the feeding grounds and roost of an undescribed species of peacock. He secured specimens of both sexes. These birds were so different from other peacocks that they were placed in a new genus and given the scientific name *Afropavo congensis*. Because *congensis* was native to the Congo, Chapin chose "Congo peacock" as its common name.

As might be expected, Chapin was delighted that he had found a bird unknown to science. But his greatest thrill had come at the moment he placed the feather taken from the chief's headdress against the plumage of a female Congo peacock and saw that it was an exact match.

3 Lore of the Peacock

"It is an old belief."—Lockhart

All through history, peacocks have been endowed with supernatural powers. Pliny the Elder, the great Roman naturalist, assured his reader that he would be safe from witchcraft if he inscribed the names of the sun and the moon on an amethyst and then tied the gem to his neck with peacock hair. However, Pliny did not specify where hair grew on a peacock's body.

Because the peacock was thought to be the favorite bird of Juno, queen of the gods, Romans were convinced that it could provide them with protection from sorcery and disease. Therefore, many Romans wore amulets fashioned in the form of peacocks when they prayed to Juno. But despite the fact that the peacock was held sacred to Juno, wealthy Romans did not hesitate to serve peafowl, roasted in their feathers, at banquets. Most of the guests at these feasts convinced themselves that they were eating a great delicacy when served peacock tongues. This was because they believed in the adage—still powerful among housewives throughout the world—that food pleasing to the eye must be delicious. Actually, peacock tongues are gristly and the bird's flesh is extremely tough.

 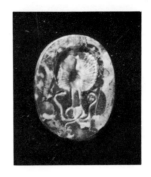

Carved by a Greek artisan centuries before the birth of Christ, this gem depicts a peacock crushing two entwined cobras.

Like the Romans, certain Eastern peoples have great respect for the peacock's potent powers. According to the *Kama Sutra*, an ancient Hindu text, a peacock bone covered with gold and tied to the right hand will make a man irresistible to women. The Bhils of central India—who venerate the peacock—regard it as all-powerful. While the entire tribe holds the bird in awe, it is especially feared by the peacock clan. The members of this clan are convinced that they will suffer greatly if they accidentally step on a peacock's track while hunting in the jungle. Women of the clan are so fearful of the peacock's magic that they immediately cover their faces when they hear one cry.

On the other hand, the Moslems of Java have little respect for the peacock and claim it is unclean. Their dislike for the bird is based on their conviction that, when the world was young, the peacock was assigned the task of guarding the gates of Paradise but neglected its duty and allowed Satan to enter. Once inside, the Devil successfully plotted the downfall of Adam and Eve.

In both the Old and New Worlds, it is considered unlucky to see a peacock. The superstitious also fear the bird's call. Europeans claim that hearing a peacock cry is an omen of doom, while Thai tribesmen maintain that the bird's call will addle

20

Not only were large numbers of peacocks kept at Hera's temple at Samos but also the rulers of that island depicted both the goddess and the bird on coins. Romans honored Hera as Juno.

snake eggs. Some residents of the Far East hold that when snakes see peacocks—which prey on snakes—the reptiles immediately stretch out to full length, lie motionless, and wait to be killed. Burmese contend that it is dangerous to let peacocks come near children because the birds may peck out the youngsters' eyes, mistaking them for the precious stones the birds are said to swallow.

In England, the notion that peacocks bring misfortune is widespread. A leading candy manufacturer discovered this when he packaged chocolates in a tin box embossed with a peacock. The item did not sell.

Formerly, peacock feathers were part of the distinctive headdress worn by servants in Russia. But in the China of yesteryear, peacock feathers were ceremoniously awarded to nobles who had faithfully served the emperor. However, in most countries, peacock feathers are considered unlucky. In the United States and Europe, not only are the bird's feathers held to be a symbol of vain glory but also the credulous claim that they are emblems of the evil eye and bring bad luck.

Actors on both sides of the Atlantic firmly believe that any play in which peacock feathers are used to decorate the stage

21

or costumes will fail. Because the feathers are said to bring disease or death, displaying them in one's home is thought to be a dangerous practice in parts of the United States. Many rural southerners are positive that if a girl keeps peacock feathers in her room, she will never marry. These individuals also maintain that if a wedding is held in a room in which peacock feathers are kept, the marriage will be an unhappy one.

No one knows why peacock feathers are thought to be unlucky. However, the origin of the superstition well may be the belief that Juno—who had a well-deserved reputation for spitefulness—punished those who dared pluck feathers from her favorite bird.

Roman mythology details how Juno beautified the peacock. The queen of the gods—so legend states—scattered the eyes of Argos, the hundred-eyed giant, over the peacock's tail after he was killed. Meanwhile, because Juno supposedly ruled the heavens, her worshipers linked the "stars" in the bird's train to those in the sky. The Romans borrowed all these beliefs from the Greeks, who held the peacock sacred to Hera, their most important goddess.

Besides playing an important part in Greek and Roman religion, the peacock was sacrificed to Odin, chief god of early Nordic peoples. The bird is also prominent in the legends of the Sannins, the supernatural immortals of Japan. But the greatest reverence has been paid to the peacock by the Hindus, who associate it with several of their gods. Among these are Indra, ruler of winds and rain, and Kartikeya, general of the celestial armies who rides a peacock across the heavens. Representations of Suraswat, patroness of learning, music, and poetry, show her, lute in hand, mounted on a peacock.

A number of Indian tribes pay special homage to the peacock. This is particularly true of the jungle-dwelling Saros.

Representations of Kartikeya, general of the celestial army, mounted on a peacock. Kartikeya is but one of many Hindu gods associated with the peacock.

When Saros tribesmen erect a temporary shrine during a religious festival, they always place a wooden peacock on the roof to guard the shrine from harm. During ceremonies honoring Galbesum, a malevolent god who destroys the livestock of those who displease him, the Saros sacrifice peacocks. They also dance around a stuffed peacock fastened to a pole.

Peacocks have learned to beg from pious Hindus. Because the peacock is held to be the companion of gods, pilgrims to holy places throughout India gladly feed the large flocks of peacocks that gather near temples. But strangely enough, an ancient Hindu text dealing with reincarnation shows little regard for the bird. It warns that those who steal vegetables will return to Earth in the form of peacocks.

Christianity has also made use of the peacock. Because it was

23

once widely believed that peacock flesh did not decay, early Christians employed the bird as the symbol of immortality. They also used the "eyes" in the train to represent the "all-seeing eye" of God. Considered an emblem of the Supreme Being, peacocks were embroidered on ecclesiastical garments. The peacocks frequently found on the walls of ancient Christian catacombs personify the souls of the faithful drinking from the Fountain of Life.

During the Middle Ages, the "Vow of the Peacock" was a rite known in every feudal castle. With hand extended over a peacock roasted in its feathers, a knight would solemnly swear "to God, to the Virgin-Saint, and to the ladies, and to the peacock" that he would perform some daring deed. After giving this pledge—failure to accomplish the chosen task meant dishonor—the knight carved up the bird and gave a piece of its flesh to all present.

Modern Saros tribesmen can appreciate why knights made a vow in the name of the peacock. The most sacred oath a Saros can make is to "swear by the peacock."

Archaeologists—students of past human life and activities—recently unearthed a bark slab in India on which was scratched a formula that supposedly cured a long list of ills. Among the ingredients were the left eye of a duck, the head of a snake, and ground-up feathers of peacock.

Even today, many residents of the Far East rely on medicines containing peacock feathers to ease pain and to restore health. In India, wearing a peacock feather or drinking the water in which one has been dipped is considered the best method of reducing a fever. While a number of hill and jungle tribes maintain that smoking a peacock feather is an antidote for snake venom, the Saros burn the bird's feathers to prevent smallpox.

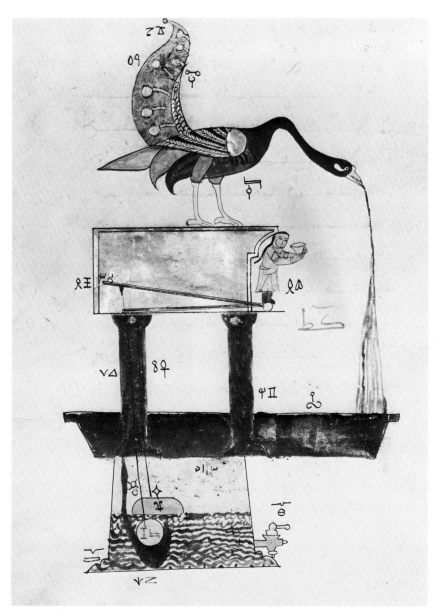

Automon in the form of a peacock from The Book of the Knowledge of ingenious Geometrical Contrivances *compiled by Al-Jazari in* A.D. *1206. This apparatus for washing the hands was probably originally used for religious purposes.*

During epidemics in India, local shamen sweep the sickness out of their villages with brooms made of peacock feathers. Because the feathers are said to have the power to extract foreign substances from human flesh, shamen use them to brush patients whose illness is thought to be the result of sorcery. Conversely, sorcerers also recognize the power of peacock feathers. Thus Nag-pa—the Tibetan magician who combats disease-carrying demons—wears peacock feathers in his tall conical hat made of yak hair.

Throughout the Orient, practitioners of folk medicine claim that peacock bills compounded into a salve will heal snake bite. They also hold that peacock flesh will draw poisons. In Sri Lanka, the Singhalese firmly believe that nostrums, pills, and ointments containing peacock feathers will cure rheumatism, aid sprains, and dislocations, and reduce swellings. The Singhalese are also convinced that sufferers from snake bite will recover if they cut an "eye" out of a peacock's train, wrap it in a plantain leaf, and smoke it three times.

Strangely enough, the eyespots in the train are not credited with helping to heal swollen or inflamed eyes. But sore eyes can be relieved, so it is claimed, by swallowing a peacock crest that has been ground into a fine powder.

Literature is crammed with references to the peacock. One of the earliest is in the Bible, where we are told that King Solomon's navy brought him "gold and silver, ivory, and apes, and peacocks." Early authors were enthralled with the bird's plumage. For example, Dionysius, a Greek scholar of the seventh century B.C., likens the peacock's feathers to "golden flowers" and calls attention to the eyes "that gleam along the train like stars."

In the third century B.C., Aelian, an early naturalist, recorded his detailed observations of peacocks bred in Rome. Not only

Cyrus the Great, LEFT, *arrayed in embroidered Persian robe.*
RIGHT, *Alexander the Great thought the peacock a magnificent bird.*

did he credit the peacock with being the most attractive of
birds but also he claimed that "the varied beauty of its plumage
surpasses the robes of the Medes and the embroideries of the
Persians." Aelian supported his statements by calling his readers'
attention to the reaction of Alexander the Great when he first
saw a peacock. Alexander was so taken by the bird's beautiful
appearance he decreed that anyone who killed a peacock would
be severely punished.

Medieval authors made good use of the peacock's haughty
manner and compared vain and proud individuals to the bird.
Shakespeare employed the same device. He also likened those
who wore gaudy clothes to peacocks. The seeming arrogance
of the peacock and its brilliant coloration have inspired other
authors and poets, including William Cowper, Paul Laurence
Dunbar, Thomas Hood, Edward Lytton, Edith Sitwell, Ed-
mund Spenser, and Robert Louis Stevenson.

27

The peacock has long been the central figure in yarns told by tribal storytellers. For example, Aesop's account of the peacock's failure to be elected king of the birds was borrowed from an ancient Far Eastern folktale. Equally ancient is the Japanese legend of a heavenly peacock that dances to music furnished by a nightingale. Peacocks have no time for dancing in the stories told by the Kurds of Turkey. The birds are too busy performing wondrous deeds.

However, in most yarns the peacock is held up to ridicule due to its disdainful walk and piercing voice. Typical of these stories, which always depict the peacock as conceited, is an old Buddhist tale in which the beautiful daughter of the king of the ducks received her father's permission to choose her own husband. All the birds formed a line and marched before the princess but she showed no interest until the peacock strutted by, when she announced, "The peacock will be my husband."

Overjoyed, the peacock spread his train and began to sing and dance. The well-brought-up princess was shocked at the bird's bad manners—his horrible voice also gave her a headache—and she whispered to her father that she could not marry such a vain boor.

King Duck congratulated his daughter on her good judgment and sent the peacock back to the jungle. To help his daughter forget her headache, he introduced her to a handsome young drake and suggested that he would make an excellent husband.

The princess—so the story goes—took her father's suggestion. As is to be expected, the princess and the drake lived happily ever after.

Peacocks, real and imaginary, have long posed for artists and inspired craftsmen. Not only did the jewelers of ancient Rome make peacock amulets of silver and gold but also they designed representations of the bird that were studded with precious stones.

Lid from early Greek vase features a finial fashioned in the form of a male peacock.

Decorated with a displaying peacock, this pottery lamp burnt olive oil. Such lamps were used wherever olives were grown in ancient times.

Mosaic from the floor of the home of the Roman governor of North Africa. Assembled by an unknown artisan in the fourth century, it depicts the birds found in the governor's garden.

Published in 1850, this polka takes its name from the legendary egotism of the peacock.

Peacocks were also featured on Roman coins. In North Africa, the bird was the favorite subject of the artisans who fashioned mosaic floors in the villas of Roman officials. The floor of a fifth-century Byzantine basilica in the ancient settlement of Tabghah near the Sea of Galilee has a mosaic representing the miracle of the loaves and fishes. The mosaic depicts not only a basket of bread and two small "charming and rather humorous" fishes but also a peacock.

Early sculptors also depicted the peacock. The main gateway of Gitta Vecchia, the ancient capital of the island of Malta, is typical. It shows Juno, the protectress of Malta, with a peacock.

Because of the peacock's place in Christian lore, medieval painters often included it in their religious works. But while Giovanni Bellini, J. van Corneliez, Carlo Crivelli, G. dai Libri, Fra Filippo Lippi, Antonello Da Messina, and Jan van Eyck pictured peacocks with saints and the Holy Family, modern painters have concentrated on capturing the bird's beauty in oil and water colors. J. A. Weir's *Peacock Feather* and John La Farge's *Peacock and Peonies* are examples of such paintings.

Proverbs do not treat the peacock kindly. Most popular sayings disparage the bird or employ it to personify false pride and ostentation. "Proud as a peacock" is found in most languages. Nearly as widespread are "conceited as a peacock," and "vain as a peacock."

A few peacock proverbs are not derogatory. The Hindustani "Who has seen the peacock dance in the forest?" is used to express regret when a man of great ability displays his talents to those totally unable to appreciate his worth. Similarly, the Malayan "Like a peacock displaying in the jungle" refers to beauty being wasted. Individuals who act in a superior manner are the targets of the Persian "The jackal dipped himself in indigo and then thought he was a peacock."

31

Certain of these proverbs may be the source of the obsolete English verb "to peacock," meaning "to show off" or "to put on airs." Common speech has also borrowed from peacock proverbs and employs the bird to denote vanity. In his *Rules for Civility*, George Washington admonished his readers, "Play not the peacock looking everywhere about you, to see if you be well deck't."

Perhaps the most unusual use of the word "peacock" was made by George III of England after his partial recovery from one of his frequent periods of insanity. The tutor assigned to help His Majesty learn the speech the king's ministers wished him to deliver at the opening of Parliament discovered that, for some unknown reason, George insisted on adding "peacock" to the end of every sentence.

The tutor was an extremely clever man. He convinced the king that, while royalty had the right to end a sentence with "peacock," the word should not be heard by commoners. Therefore, the tutor warned, George must softly whisper "peacock" when addressing his subjects. His Royal Highness agreed, and the pauses caused by his murmuring "peacock" to himself made the speech most effective.

4 *Physical Characteristics*

*"He who is of bad nature sees nothing in
the peacock but its ugly feet."*—Sadi

There is nothing commonplace about the appearance of the common or blue peacock. The male of this species has a metallic bluish-green head and neck relieved by white patches above and below the eyes, while a spoon-shaped crest composed of blue-tipped brushlike feathers crowns the head. The brown wings are mottled with black, the body feathers are gray, those on the back have cinnamon bars, and those on the underparts are barred with buff.

Female blue peacocks are more conservatively dressed than their mates. The hens have chestnut heads, white throats and forenecks, and brownish-black breasts tinged with green. Underparts are buff, while the feathers on the back are brown, sprinkled with buff.

Because the green or Javan peacock has longer legs and a more extended and thinner neck than its Indian kin, it gives the impression of being much larger. Green peacocks show practically no difference between the plumage of males and females. Both sexes have lustrous turquoise-and-black wings,

33

There is little difference in the plumage of both sexes of green peacock except that the female has no train. Note the elongated neck and long crest of this female.

while their bodies are predominately green, mottled with bronze from crest to tail. The crest consists of a bundle of long, erect, spiky, bright green feathers.

Naturalists cannot agree on whether the blue and green coloration of the peacock provides it with an effective camouflage. It is difficult to settle the debate because the birds rarely make any attempt to hide. Their excellent hearing and extremely keen eyes enable them to detect danger before it comes close, so they usually have ample time to fly to safety.

Blue and green peacocks do not fly as well as the African species. Nevertheless, they have the ability to "take off" quickly and rise rapidly at a sharp angle to the ground. Females can engage in a continuous series of flights, each covering several hundred yards. Males, handicapped by the weight of their trains, are more earthbound. Thus it is possible for a group of fleet hunters to run down a male that has been "grounded" in open country by the weight of its plumage.

Because blue and green peacocks are long legged, they often find it difficult to keep their balance when the wind hits their outspread fans. When this happens, the birds dance about, reel to the left and right, posture and strut. These actions have led to the accusation that peacocks are vain, while, in reality, all they are doing is trying to stay on their feet.

Buffeted by wind, a displaying male may stubbornly keep his fan spread and try to remain upright by firmly bracing his large ugly feet. Incidentally, all through history, ridicule has been heaped on the peacock's feet. But if East Indian tradition is true, this was not always so. According to legend, the peacock once had beautiful legs and feet but was cheated out of them by a partridge that persuaded the peacock to change

A male peacock displaying in a high wind is often unsteady on his feet.

Male, roosting, and female Congo peacocks. Note the banded feathers on the female—Chapin's means of identification.

with him during a dancing contest and then flew away.

Except for the color of their plumage, blue and green peacocks closely resemble one another, but the Congo peacock's physical characteristics differ greatly from those of its Asian relatives. Unlike both *cristatus* and *muticus*, the Congo peacock is not a large bird. As a matter of fact, males of this species are midgets when placed beside either a mature male blue or green peacock. This is due to more than the body size. Male Congo peacocks—along with all female peafowl—lack trains.

In comparison to its colorful kin, the Congo peacock is dowdy. The trainless male has a broad short tail, a partly bare neck that displays a patch of red skin, a large feather tuft on the beak, and a double black-and-white crest. As noted, male

Congo peacocks have an iridescent blackish plumage while females are reddish-brown and black.

Afropavo congensis may be the most unattractive of the peacocks but it has one rare distinction. It is the only pheasant to originate outside Asia.

Ever since bird fanciers discovered that blue and green peacocks will interbreed in captivity, they have devoted considerable effort to developing uniquely colored peacocks. Among these mutations are albino, pied, and black-shouldered strains.

Blue peacock and some color mutations developed by bird fanciers. Note colorless eye spots on the albino peacock's train. Pied peacock, bottom left; iris peacock, perching, right.

Perhaps the most beautiful of these is the albino, which has never been found in the wild state. A perfect specimen of this strain lacks the slightest trace of pigment. However, when the train is spread and the light is just right, every detail of the eye pattern can be seen, "appearing and reappearing like the successive ripples in watered silk."

5 Ways of the Peacock

"Small habits well pursued . . ."—More

Generally speaking, blue, green, and Congo peacocks have the same habits. Thus, in the pages that follow, unless special attention is directed to a dissimilarity, it should be understood that the behavior pattern being discussed is identical in the three species.

Peacocks have been called the most sedentary of birds. They have earned this distinction because they rarely move far from an area where food is abundant, water plentiful, and a suitable roost available. However, if the birds are disturbed, they will desert their usual haunts for several days. The only other time they travel any distance is when drought dries up their drinking places or at the start of the breeding season when the males take their harems into the jungle, mate, and raise their families.

Creatures of habit, peacocks have regular feeding grounds and return to the same roost every night. They also go to the same place to seek shelter from the sun every day. While partially overgrown jungle clearings serve many peacocks as "sunshades," most peacocks prefer to pass the heat of the day settled on a well-shaded branch just above the ground. Here

A blue peacock roosts in the Cincinnati Zoo, affording a good view of the short tail feathers below the long coverts.

they take a nap or preen. Frequently, only the male in a family group squats on the branch. He does not sleep but keeps careful watch while his hens take dust baths and rest.

Despite the fact that blue peacocks avoid intense heat, they can withstand extremely high temperatures. William Beebe, world-famous authority on the Phasianidae, observed peacocks in India following their normal routine when the thermometer recorded 147°F. Interestingly enough, although the blue peacock is a tropical bird, it suffers little discomfort from the frost, snow, and cold of temperate regions. On the other hand, the green peacocks that are allowed to roam freely in public parks and on the lawns of large estates must be provided with a warm shelter during the winter months in regions where the temperature drops. Actually, few green peacocks are exhibited uncaged. This is not solely because of their dislike of the cold. Green peacocks have vile tempers. While male blue peacocks rarely fight except at the start of the breeding season, male green peacocks do not get along with one another at any time. Moreover, it is not unusual for both males and females of this species to become aggressive toward people.

Peacocks are omnivorous. Their varied menu includes frogs, grubs, mice, small lizards, snakes, and worms. In India, the blue peacock is protected not only for religious reasons but also because it delights in dining on young cobras. Indeed, there seems to be nothing edible that peacocks will not taste. But while the birds eat a considerable amount of meat, they probably would be content with a vegetarian diet consisting of bamboo shoots, grass, and grains supplemented with berries, buds, seeds, and flower petals that have either fallen or can be plucked from low shrubs. Peacocks feed only on the ground although they will, like chickens, snap at flies and chase butterflies.

41

In their search for food, peacocks frequently raid cultivated fields. This is particularly true in those areas where peacocks are protected. Birds raised for ornamental purposes often display a preference for the plants in their owner's gardens rather than their usual diet of bread, table scraps, and scientifically compounded feed. Proof that hungry peacocks can as easily ruin a formal garden as they can wipe out the simple planting of a jungle tribesman is furnished by an early nineteenth-century writer who obviously had little regard for the birds. Perhaps a peacock had destroyed some of his prized plants when he wrote: "I find nothing that is either pleasing or deserving of attention, except a beautiful plumage. Its voice is a loud and disgusting scream, and the damage it does to the plants in our gardens is scarcely compensated by its elegant appearance there."

Normally, peacocks begin to feed immediately after awakening, although they may first go to a stream to drink. On the way to the water, the hens usually form compact groups but frequently break away to snare an insect or to pluck a leaf. Males walk some distance behind the females, constantly watching for danger.

In those parts of India where peacocks are highly regarded, the birds are not so alert to possible peril. Eventually they become semi-tame and, as they lose their fear of man, depend upon cultivated crops for food and spend most of the day in garden plots.

Truly wild peacocks always feed in the open so that they can more easily detect an intruder or other threat to their safety and make their escape. While peacocks occasionally run for cover when disturbed, they prefer to make their retreat in the air.

Because peacocks are so wary, it is practically impossible for even experienced trackers to stalk them in their native haunts.

The peacock is the national bird of India. There albino peacocks are bred in captivity and become semi-tame.

The only way naturalists have been able to observe their life patterns in detail has been to conceal themselves at some vantage point with an unobstructed view and watch the birds' activities through powerful field glasses.

While it is no easy task to get within sight of either a blue or green peacock, field zoologists have found it far more difficult to learn the ways and wiles of the Congo peacock. *Congensis* is not a common bird, although it probably was once widely distributed in the jungles of the Congo. Wholesale trapping by

Congo peacocks may vanish in the wild but the chance of their becoming extinct is remote. They breed freely in captivity. Here a mated pair is being shipped to a zoo.

Pygmies has reduced its range, and presently the Congo peacock is found only in certain thickly wooded uplands—a terrain students of birds have found formidable—that have little chance of being flooded. Even those ornithologists who have entered the Congo peacock's habitat rarely have encountered a specimen. This is partially due to the fact that this species is one of the shyest of birds. Moreover, although Congo peacocks roam the forest floor in pairs seeking fruits that have dropped from trees, they are difficult to see. This is because they take great pains to stay in the shadows.

As indicated, peacocks do not mind being seen, providing they are in a position that enables them to notice an intruder first. This explains why these birds roost in tall, isolated trees with smooth bark that offers few footholds to nocturnal predators. The trees selected have branches only near the top, and the lowest of these is used as a perch. This limb is always devoid of leaves. As a result, the roosting peacocks can see in all directions.

44

Roosting procedures differ slightly in the three species but all peacocks get ready to roost shortly before dusk. Male blue peacocks lead their harems to the group's roosting tree, but no hen dares fly into it. First, the harem has to wait patiently while the male walks about, cocks his head, listens, and peers this way and that. When satisfied that all is well, he makes several false starts and then, finally, soars upward at an acute angle and lands on the sleeping limb. A male expends considerable energy in this flight, and, when it is over, can be heard to grunt like "a workman wielding a heavy sledge."

A few minutes later the hens rise to the roost but their flight is not spectacular. Once on the bough, the females keep shifting position and moving back and forth. Meanwhile, the male continues to listen and to look on every side. Eventually he is convinced that the group is in no danger and drops his stiff,

When frightened, blue peacocks rocket into the air in a sharply angled takeoff, as shown in an old print from a nineteenth-century book.

erect, "lookout" posture. Now the birds settle down, face the same way, and nestle together.

Peacocks are very early risers. They leave the roost before sunup—the male in the lead—in a graceful swoop that carries them a considerable distance from the tree. If it has rained during the night, the birds remain in their roost until the sun has dried the ground and their plumage. While waiting to feed, they preen their feathers, stretch, and shake their wings. But even after they and their surroundings are dry, the hens make no attempt to go foraging until the male zooms to the ground.

Green peacocks—which often roost in low trees in open jungle—do not engage in fancy aerial acrobatics to reach their sleeping perch. Instead of making a single flight, they get there in stages. They rise into a tree that stands close to the tree in which they roost, make a short flight to the top of another tree that is even closer, then fly onto the perch. This simple step-by-step ascent contrasts greatly with the birds' descent the following morning. After fluttering their wings for a few beats, the birds start a long slide to the ground and, just before reaching it, rapidly flutter their wings again. The gracefulness of this maneuver is frequently marred if the birds are thrown off course by the branches of bushes just before landing.

Not only do blue and green peacocks differ in the way they reach their roosts but also they do not have the same sleeping arrangements. Only the immature of the green peacock crowd close together and sleep side by side, as do blue peacocks of all ages.

Because Congo peacocks fly with great skill, they have little

Many ornithologists consider the green or Javan peacock the most beautiful of gallinaceous birds. Here, a male and female perch in a low tree near their watering place.

47

trouble reaching their lofty roosts. But these birds, which are more or less silent during the day, spend almost as much time calling at night as they do sleeping. They have two cries: *rro-ho-ho-o-ah*, followed by *gowe-gowah*, which may be repeated as much as thirty times at one calling. During the night the calls increase in volume, and the noise made by individual birds and family groups can be heard for miles.

Even the noise of a falling branch will prompt every peacock within hearing to call. Not only is the Indian peacock's *kok-kok-kok-kok!* unmusical but also it is powerful. Equally loud is the raucous, wailing alarm call of male blue peacocks. This cry frequently pierces the stillness of the jungle because it is not only sounded when danger threatens but also just before the birds roost. Female peacocks also have unattractive voices except when "talking" to their chicks but they are not as noisy as their mates.

Despite folk belief, peacocks do not sound this alarm call to warn other creatures. Actually, peacocks have no association with their neighbors. Nor do the birds fear most predators. The sharp spurs and pugnacity of the peacock provide it with a strong defense against enemies. However, civets, jackals, and hawk eagles kill peacocks with ease. Blue peacocks are so afraid of hawk eagles that they constantly look upward while feeding. If they see a hawk eagle in the sky they run for cover rather than take to the air as they normally do.

As indicated, male peacocks court every female they encounter. Whether a male displays his fan for a few seconds or for well over an hour, he "dances" a few steps at a time, turning slightly to the left and right on his sturdy white legs. But most hens give no sign that they are impressed with either the dancing or the unfolding of the fan. They continue to look for food and seemingly have absolutely no interest in mating.

48

Sooner or later, however, a female draws close to her ardent suitor. As she approaches, the male turns his back on her. This forces the female to run around the male in order to face him. This procedure may take place several times before the male starts to peck the ground just in front of him. Naturalists are convinced that this activity corresponds to an act of courtship performed by many close relatives of the peacock—the presentation of food by the male to the female.

As the male continues to peck the ground, the coy female comes closer and closer. In time, she reaches the spot where the "food" is, crouches down, and the birds mate.

Sometimes a courting male will walk backward toward the hen he is trying to impress and rapidly turn around to show the splendor of his erected train. But he may regret approaching a hen in this fashion—unable to see behind, he has no warning if a rival decides to take advantage of an excellent target.

Courting male's exposed rump becomes a target for a rival.

The frequent attempts of both hens and chicks to raise and spread a fan in imitation of the male is most amusing. Hens try to make a fan with their undersized tail coverts, while the chicks vigorously vibrate their wings and erect their undeveloped tail feathers.

Chicks attempting to spread their tail coverts well may be instinctively imitating older birds. When the hens erect their tails and boldly attack anything that threatens their young, they may be copying the posturing of male peacocks before a fight.

While it is most enjoyable to see a tiny chick try to raise a fan, watching a family group of peacocks play "tag" is a far more fascinating experience. Usually, only immature birds play the game, which consists of chasing one another in anticlockwise circles around a bush. But adult birds have been known to join the youngsters. Even more infrequently, males whose trains have molted unite with the others and run rapidly around the bush. The game comes to a sudden end when, without warning, all the players scatter in different directions.

6 Family Life

"The pecok, with his aungels fethres brighte."—Chaucer

In order to attract mates, over half the known species of birds burst into song. While the melody, rhythm, volume, and pitch of this musical courting varies from species to species, it is, in most instances, pleasing to the human ear. This is not true of the peacock's love song. Its voice is just as raucous during the breeding season as it is at any other time of the year. Indeed, the cries of a male peacock seeking hens for his harem seem especially strident—probably because amorous males are especially noisy.

Generally speaking, blue and green peacocks start to breed at the onset of the rainy season, which begins about the time the males are in full feather after their annual molt.

About a month or two after their plumage is completely restored, male blue and green peacocks begin calling. Blue peacocks serenade females with a meowing *ming-ao*—a cry jungle tribesmen claim is the birds' way of saying "there will be rain." As a matter of fact, peacocks do call more frequently before thunderstorms. Green peacocks do not meow to catch the attention of hens but trumpet a penetrating *hah-o-hah.*

51

A blue or Indian peacock displays for a female

Once males corral a harem, they rarely call. But the jungle still resounds to the peacock's mating cries. These calls are made by young males that cannot compete with their elders for females. Not only are their voices less strong and their fans not as showy but also they are no match for them in a fight. This does not prevent them from making advances to hens, however. Young males not only call all day but also at night. Like all anxious swains, they are particularly persistent when the moon is full. If they do manage to gain a female's affection, a mature male will probably break up the engagement.

As indicated, male green peacocks cannot tolerate one another. Therefore, they often fight to the death over a hen. Also, although blue male peacocks usually get along very well, they do fight during the breeding season. However, first they may try to intimidate a rival by displaying their trains and strutting. If this bluff does not work, the two birds join battle, but their contests are not so vicious as those of green peacocks.

Fighting peacocks slash and parry with their strong legs as they try to sink their spurs into an opponent's flesh. At times the birds may rise as high as ten feet in the air, striking with both legs and pecking with their beaks as feathers fly in all directions. The struggle ends when the defeated male, his breast torn and feathers tattered, runs away. But if retreat does not satisfy the proud victor, he may chase his would-be rival and renew the battle.

Peacocks are not outstanding architects. Their nests are usually either hollows a foot across and two inches deep scratched in bare ground and lined with a few dried leaves or natural depressions in the ground. Nor do the birds display great building skill when they nest on weathered stumps or in a crotch between two low branches—favorite nesting sites of the green peacock.

Although peacocks show little ingenuity in making their nests, they exhibit considerable proficiency in hiding them. Their preferred nesting sites are clumps of tall grass, stands of bamboo, and overgrown shrubbery. Many peacocks prefer to nest in marshlands.

While blue peacocks are especially skilled at hiding their nests, they may not attempt to conceal them in areas where they are protected by man and have no fear of predators. Meanwhile, their nests are found on the tops of deserted native huts and the caved-in roofs of moss-covered ruins. They also sublet the abandoned nests of birds of prey.

The number of eggs laid varies with the species. Blue peacock hens deposit from three to eight eggs in their nests. There are records of as many as fifteen eggs being found at one

A pair of blue peacock chicks bred at the San Diego Zoo

time, but naturalists are convinced that this was a double laying
—two hens building one nest, both laying their eggs in it, and
one doing the incubating. This is not unusual among fowl-like
birds.

Protected semidomesticated peacocks lay more eggs and
raise more chicks than wild birds. This is because few of the
young fall prey to predators, and the parents have little diffi-
culty in securing enough food for them.

Pitted with tiny pores, a blue peacock's large, thick-shelled,
glossy, broad, oval eggs are more or less pointed at the smaller
end. The eggs may vary in color, although all the eggs in a set
are normally the same hue. However, one may be lime white,
another a rosy buff or the color of coffee mixed with a large
amount of milk. A number of eggs may be speckled with reddish-

brown markings, particularly at the larger ends.

Green peacocks lay larger eggs than their kin. Their four to six eggs are never spotted and range in color from a dull white to a rich cream. This species rarely raises more than two chicks.

Eggs are incubated for twenty-eight days. When the babies hatch, their flight feathers can be seen and they develop so rapidly that the youngsters can make ragged flights to low branches when about a week old. By the time they are a month old, most of their plumage and their crests have appeared. But it may take as much as six years for a male's train to reach its maximum length.

Hens feed their broods from their beaks at which the chicks instinctively peck. But on game farms where peacock eggs are given to barnyard hens to hatch, the babies learn to pick up food from the ground. If orphaned chicks are placed in the care of an immature female peacock, she is stimulated to feed them when the youngsters peck at her beak.

Male blue and green peacocks pay no more attention to their chicks than they do to the building of the nest. But when their offspring are well developed, hens, immatures, and the male are united in a family group.

Interestingly enough, although blue and green peacocks are polygamous in the wild, they do not seem to miss their harems in captivity. Captive males may even help feed chicks.

As the breeding season of the Congo peacock approaches, the necks of the males turn a bright red, while featherless spots on the skins of the hens take on a vivid orange-red hue. Because this species is monogamous, the males do not have to engage in a series of courtships. Nor is their wooing as spectacular as that of their Asian relatives. Lack of a train means that male Congo peacocks can only raise and spread a small fan when displaying. Hens also erect their tail feathers as the male drops his wings.

A Congo peacock chick bred at the Bronx Zoo

Congo peacocks have no real nest but deposit their two light-cream to red-brown eggs in a moss-covered tree fork or in a hollow stump. The female incubates the eggs for approximately four weeks while the male stands guard. If threatened, the female crouches and hides her head under a wing and looks "deceptively like a moss tussock."

Babies remain under their mother for two days after hatching. They then flutter to the ground where their father welcomes them with a high bell-like call. Once the chicks have left the nest, they do not return to it. They spend the night following their first trip to the ground under the male's breast feathers. Thereafter, they sleep on a branch huddled close to the hen, who tries to cover all of her brood with her wings.

The chicks grow quickly, and when only six days old can make flights of twenty feet. They leave their parents when they are four and a half months old and, about ten months later, start raising families of their own.

56

7 Peacock and Man

"Remember that the most beautiful things in the world are the most useless; peacocks and lilies for instance."—Ruskin

Pity the poor peacock! It is no longer the prized treasure of kings who thought nothing of spending vast sums on the up-keep of flocks of these birds. Then, too, domestic fowl and roast beef have replaced the peacock as the main dishes at banquets.

The peacock began to lose its prestige as the Middle Ages drew to a close. Actively engaged in opening trade routes and waging war in hopes of acquiring more land, the rulers of Europe had neither the time nor the money to squander on ornamental birds. Moreover, fickle fashion declared that pea-cock feathers were no longer stylish and dictated that they be replaced with ostrich plumes.

By the late eighteenth century, the peacock had fallen into disrepute. This decline in popularity was undoubtedly hastened by the importation of green peacocks into Europe. The arrival of this nasty-tempered species gave all peacocks a bad name. But more importantly, great changes were taking place and old values were giving way to new ones on both sides of the Atlantic. No bird—even one as splendid as the peacock—

Princess Kaiulani, heir to the throne of the Hawaiian Islands, was very fond of peacocks and often had her dressmaker use the birds' feathers to decorate her evening gowns. Kaiulani would have ruled over the Islands if they had not been annexed by the United States in 1898.

could possibly enchant the American colonists who had repudiated their king or the French citizens who beheaded theirs. Nor did the peacock have any allure for the philosophers who suggested that the time had come for thinking men to plan the world of the future. Peacocks were forgotten as scholars debated how to insure that future generations would not know war, injustice, or hunger.

Historians call the period in which social and political ideals dominated the writings and speeches of learned individuals the "Age of Reason." This era has had a tremendous influence on modern thought. It also wiped out the last vestige of admiration for the peacock. The Age of Reason could not tolerate a useless thing of beauty.

58

"A Girl Feeding Peacocks," an oil painting by the famous British artist Frederic, Lord Leighton (1830–1896). In the mid-nineteenth century the beauty of the useless peacock became a symbol of revolt against industrialism.

Strangely enough, it was the "uselessness" of the peacock that brought it back into favor in the mid-nineteenth century. By then the dire effects of the Industrial Revolution were apparent. Smoke poured from factory chimneys, polluting the air, skilled craftsmen were giving way to machines designed for mass production, and "objects of unparalleled ugliness were pouring out of the mills."

No one was more appalled at these conditions than a group of English artists and writers called the Pre-Raphaelites. Maintaining that it made no difference whether an object was useful or useless as long as it was beautiful, they chose the peacock as a symbol of their revolt against industrialism.

Today, peacocks still strut majestically across the greenswards of public parks and private estates. As has been reflected through the centuries, man has an unusual relationship with the bird, harboring mixed emotions about it. But one thing is certain—many farmers who see their crops destroyed by peacocks do not revere the bird or admire its beauty, and would rejoice if the peacock were to become extinct.

They may get their wish. As tree after tree in the African rain forest falls to meet the world's demand for lumber, the chances that the Congo peacock will survive in the wild become fewer and fewer. Fortunately, these birds breed readily in captivity and thus will be preserved for future generations.

The ever increasing demand for agricultural land could, eventually, lead to the disappearance of the green peacock over much of its present range. Similarly, the clearing of the Indian jungle may, in time, leave only a few semi-tame blue peacocks to fill the early morning hours with their penetrating cries.

But even if both green and blue peacocks should be totally exterminated in the wild, there is no danger of their becoming extinct. Like the Congo peacock, these species thrive in captivity. Indeed, many zoos have peacocks they would like to dis-

Blue peacocks roam the grounds of Warwick Castle, England.

pose of but find it impossible. It is not that the birds are expensive. In ancient Greece a pair of peacocks cost 10,000 drachmas (approximately $3,500). Today, the current price for a pair of mature birds is about fifty dollars!

But even though peacocks are available at bargain prices, they are difficult to sell. As indicated, zoos are overstocked, and no individual would even consider acquiring a pair of peacocks unless he had a large estate. But wouldn't it be delightful if the lawn of the average house were big enough for a peacock promenade—then ordinary people could enjoy the beauty of the bird as did the kings of yesteryear!

Index